Sketches
of Hales Owen III

by Bill Hazlehurst

**A special millennium album with
fifty pen and ink sketches of
memorable local buildings
and scenes.**

****

QuercuS
John Roberts
67 Cliffe Way, Warwick CV34 5JG
Tel/Fax 01926 776363
****

Sketches of Hales Owen III

by Bill Hazlehurst

ISBN 1 898136 17 3

First Published 1999

The Artist

Bill's previous books include full a biography. We will just add that from three grandchildren in *Sketches of Hales Owen* (1993), the score is now two grandsons and three grandaughters.

Contents

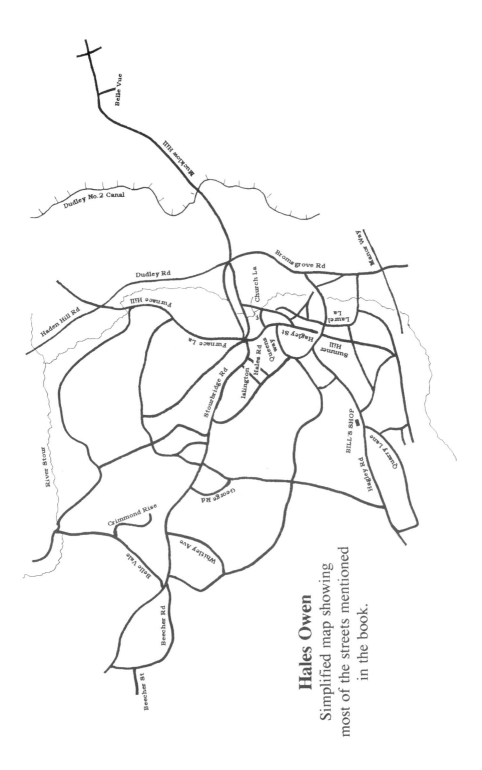

Hales Owen

Simplified map showing
most of the streets mentioned
in the book.

Introduction

Sketches of Hales Owen and *Sketches of Hales Owen II* started with a potted history of the town from mediaeval times. I will not repeat the story but would like to say something about Hales Owen as a borough because there is some mystery about it.

The town first gained borough status from King Henry III in about 1270, and it was obtained by the Abbott. Other mediaeval towns became boroughs because of a castle, a river or because they were trading centres. The fact that the Abbey achieved the Royal Charter had the disadvantage that successive Abbots were unwilling to sell any land. They regarded the land they had been granted and the feudal rights attached to it as a sacred inheritance which they could not dispose of. This lead to repeated disputes over the feudal services which the townspeople owed to the Abbey until 1327, when the Abbott agreed to replace them with a yearly payment. At last the town could begin to take advantage of the possibilities that its charter offered.

For centuries Hales Owen was governed by a Squire-Magistrate supported by the Vicar. It was not until the 19th century that any real municipal development took place. Local acts of parliament allowed committees to be set up with powers to establish police forces, street lighting and paving, but it was not until the Municipal Reform Act of 1835 that local councillors were elected. Unfortunately for Hales Owen, the Act did not list our town as a charter borough and so it did not apply. In 1876 a Royal Commission enquired into places not covered by the Act but still the status of Hales Owen was not confirmed as a borough. What had gone wrong? Was the town still a charter borough? It seemed not because another Act of Parliament in 1883 failed to mention us. It appeared that somehow charter borough status had lapsed, though no document has been found to record the event.

Towns like Hales Owen which were not covered by the Municipal Reform Act of 1835 lacked many of the essential services, especially powers to take public health measures. Relief under the Poor Law was available and managed by groups of parishes. Hales Owen belonged to the Stourbridge Union, which by implication reduced its status to that of a parish.

The Public Health Act of 1875 created new powers and regulations about sewage, water supply, nuisance, scavenging and infectious diseases. It became compulsory to have a Medical Officer of Health. However this Act only applied to boroughs and a new creation, urban district councils, and because Hales Owen was not mentioned in the 1835 Act it could not become one. Some status was achieved under another part of the 1875 Act in that membership of the Stourbridge Union of parishes enabled it to become a Rural District. This included Lye and Wollescote until 1897 and Quinton until 1910.

Hales Owen grew considerably during the late 19th and early 20th century so that in 1925 it achieved the status of urban district. Good local government and prosperity from that time finally brought it the recognition of being a borough once more on 19th September 1936.

What does Borough status mean?. It gains very little powers over that of an Urban District, who maintain highways, housing, levy and collect rates, preserving and creating culture and other amenities. It does however have rights to set and impose it's own bye laws. The Chairman of the Council becomes a Mayor and the Council Members become Aldermen. It can confer Freedom of the Borough on Citizens. Therefore as can be seen no great additional powers are gained by becoming a Borough. However it does give a civic dignity granted by Royal Approval for many years of civic work and endevour. Once gained it is cherished by the Town's people.

Our town once again lost its individual borough status in 1974 when it was merged with Stourbridge and Dudley to become part of Dudley Metropolitan Borough. To the disgust of many local people the council chamber and library were demolished and a supermarket built on the site. (One might ask, who was burning bridges?) All the Borough of Hales Owen regalia and a considerable collection of silver plate was removed to Dudley. Why? To many people this seemed like robbing them of their civic pride and that they no longer have any say or control of what happens in our ancient town.

Perhaps we should pursue the argument that we still have the Borough status granted in 1270, since no document seems to exist to disprove it. It would make no difference to the way we are governed but might restore some lost civic pride to both young and old in this homely town.

The crest shows a mural crown (that is, looking like a wall) with an anvil rising from it depicting the town's iron and steel trades. The chain represents the Cradley chain making tradition.

The shield is an arrangment of emblems from the arms of various owners of the Manor of Hales:

Earl Roger de Montgomery (1066 - 1094) - the left part of the lion rampant which would be in red,

Robert Dudley, Earl of Leicester (1555) - the right part of the lion in green on a gold ground,

The Premonstratensian Canons of Hales Owen (1218 - 1538) - the fleur de lys in gold on a blue ground,

Viscount Cobham of the Lyttleton family who have held the Manor since 1559 - the two escallops in silver,

The supporter on the left is a Canon of the Premonstratensian Order to represent the Abbott of Hales Owen. On the right is an early 15th gentleman representing Sir Thomas Lyttleton, Lord Chief Justice of the Court of Common Pleas.

The Motto reads 'Respice, aspice, prospice', meaning 'Look to the past, the present and the future.'

Many Hales Owen people think that the developments of the 1950s and 60s destroyed many of the town's attractive old buildings. This is true, but old buildings had been vanishing for many years before that. My sketches of some of them have appeared in *Sketches of Hales Owen* books I and II, so where I mention them below there are page references.

Some very old wattle and daub buildings in Birmingham Street were demolished many years ago. A half timbered house at the bottom of Great Cornbow by Telford's bridge was demolished in 1911, and the Workhouse in Church Street [HII pg 25] even earlier. The Market House [HIII pg x] went in 1800.

Buildings which could have been saved in the 1950s and 60s include the timbered house in Great Cornbow [HI pg 24]. Built in the early 1500s, it was thought to be the dower house of a French lady. Beside it was a brick Georgian house [HI pg 24] and both were removed to make space for the Swimming Pool.

Then there were the timbered cottages by the Church School gates in Church Street which some local historians believe could once have been the Plume of Feathers public house. Another very old pub was the Globe in Peckingham Street [HII pg 36] which was destroyed at about the same time.

More recently built properties which should have been preserved include the birthplace of Francis Brett Young in Laurel Lane [HI pg 78], the Police Station in New Road which would have made a splendid museum, and not forgetting the old Library and Council Chamber [HI pg 31]

As early as 1948 plans were afoot to develop the town. Reproduced here is the Christmas card from the mayor of that year, a distant aerial view of Hales Owen illustrating some of the ideas which were around. It's title, 'Prospice', is taken from the Borough's motto and means 'look to the future'. I wish they had carried out just a small part of these ideas.

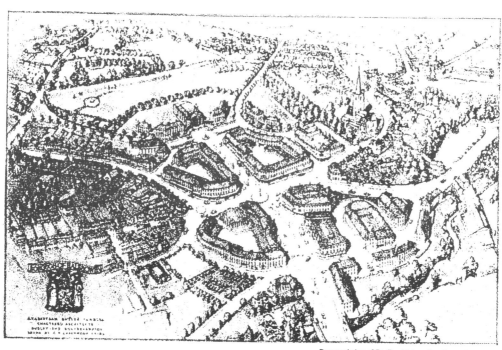

PROSPICE

By permission of Dudley Metropolitan Borough Council

6

1. The Market House

This sketch was developed from a primitive drawing by an unknown artist in 1771, the only one known to have been completed while the building still stood.

Built in 1540, the Market House stood at the top of Peckingham Street just into Little Cornbow and facing Great Cornbow. William Harris described it as a spacious building with upper rooms used for public business, in fact as a town hall. He wrote that a prison was attached together with conveniences fit for such a building.

Through neglect the Market House fell into a dilapidated state but not beyond repair. In 1800 the owner, Lord Lyttleton, offered it to the people of the town at a peppercorn rent if they agreed to carry out repairs. The offer was not accepted so the old building was demolished and the materials used to repair other properties, Harris adding 'to the eternal disgrace of the people of the Borough'.

EE·ARE·GOODE·AND·HONOURE·TE·KYNGE

The Market House, Hales Owen c.1760

8

A view of the town

9

2. A View of the Town

This leafy and rural view is from the high ground overlooking the Earl's pathway and the scene must be earlier than 1909, when the Grammar School was built. The part of the field by the wall is now occupied by the Earl's Way dual carriageway, while the rest of the field is part of the sports ground of the present Earl's High School.

3. Church of
St John the Baptist

This view of our beautiful church is from the
west. To the right is a row of trees which still
exists but the Rectory at the end was demolished some years ago.

St Johns, Hales Owen.

12

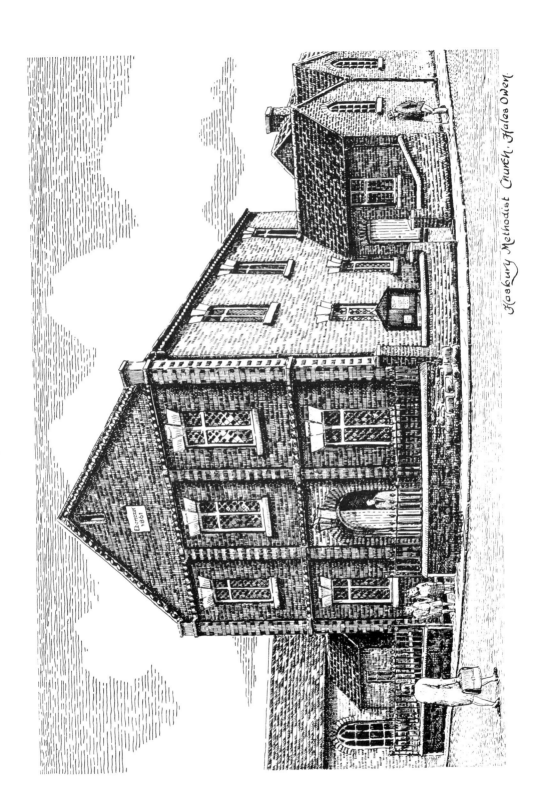

Hasbury Methodist Church, Hales Owen.

13

4. Hasbury Methodist Church

Hasbury Primitive Methodist Church had a stone on the front recording the date it was built which read 'Ebeneezer 1861'. However, members had already been meeting for some thirty years in a cottage at Cherry Tree Lane. I have been told that at one time the church had a small gasometer storing fuel to light and heat the building. The old church was replaced by a modern one in the same area.

5. Bethel Mission

This building stood on the corner of Little Cornbow next to the old Star Inn, see picture 29. It was let by a group which broke away from the Baptist Church after some obscure dispute.

The building was known as Bethel Mission long after it ceased to be a place of worship because the name could still be seen up to the time it was demolished. Most older people will remember it as the Borough Registration Office for our 'hatched, matched and despatched'.

To the left of the Mission on the corner of Great Cornbow stood the High Cross, which in 1908 was blown down in a storm and re-erected in St John's churchyard. [HII pg 11]

To the right is the Coop warehouse which probably occupied the site of the old Market House (picture 1.). With the Cross on one side and the Market House on the other it is not difficult to imagine the area as Hales Owen's market square.

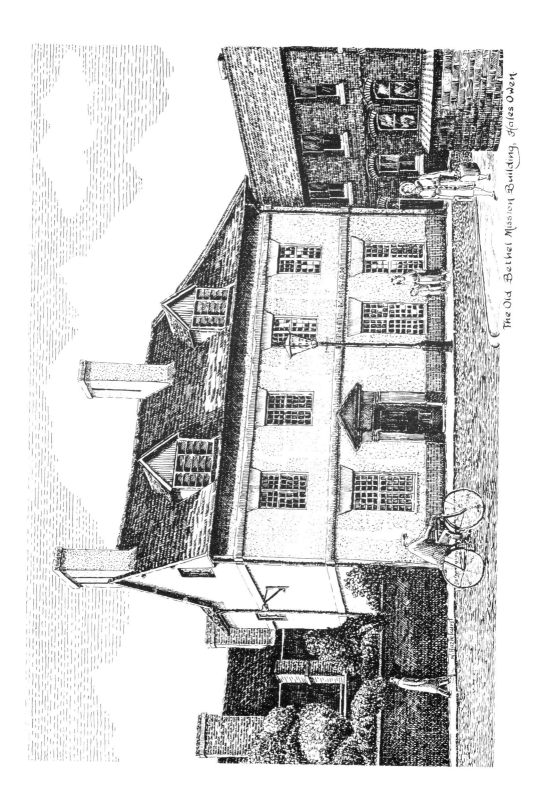

The Old Bethel Mission Building, Hales Owen

16

Belle Vale Chapel

17

6. Belle Vale Chapel

This small chapel once stood on the spare ground at the junction of Belle Vale and Crimmond Rise. My sketch shows the porch at the side of the building, moved from its original position between the front windows to allow the widening of Belle Vale. The flat roofed school rooms at the back were built by the subscriptions and labour of the congregation.

7. Saint Kenelm's Church

St Kenelm's is not really in Hales Owen, but I have included it because it was once a chapelry attached to St John's.

Long ago pilgrims would have passed through Hales Owen on their way to the holy spring at St Kenelm's, which is the source of the River Stour. The stream was thought to have healing powers.

The spring was beneath the church and reached through a door. This is the spot where the boy King of Mercia was said to have been murdered on the orders of his sister. However, the legend seems to have been confused because documents signed by King Kenelm exist, and their dates contradict the story that he died as a boy.

St Kenelm's once served the lost village of Kenelmstowe but is now the parish church of Romsley.

St. Kenelms Church, Romsley

St. Peter's Cradley

8. Saint Peter's Church

This is how we see St Peter's church, Cradley today, but it has not always looked the same. Before 1875 there was no tower, just a small turret topped with a copper cone. Originally the tower also had a turret, which was four sided with windows all round and a weather vane. This was removed in 1933 after subsidence had made repairs necessary.

The church started life in 1786 when a Wesleyan Chapel in Butcher's Lane was sold to the Reverend Thomas Best. This was dismantled and the bricks used for the foundations of a new nonconformist chapel following the Countess of Huntingdon Connection, with the Rev.d Best as Minister.

Later Thomas Best seems to have changed his religious convictions. In May 1798 he published a handbill telling the congregation and the seat holders that worship was suspended by the order of the Bishop of Worcester so that alterations could be made to conform to Church of England furnishings and practice.In September the altered church was consecrated by the Bishop and Rev.d Best was appointed perpetual curate. This left the nonconformist congregation with no place to worship. Thomas Best continued in office until he died in 1821 at the age of 61.

9. Church Lane

I said in *Sketches of Hales Owen II* that no book about the town could be complete without a sketch of Church Lane. The pictures opposite and on the next page are my contributions to this book.

This view is from Whitehall Drive. The old pubs at the top and bottom of this steep lane, the Malt Shovel and the Plough, are gone but not forgotten. Reliance Printing Works started business in one of the cottages before moving to premises in Birmingham Street.

The house at the bottom right known as Half Moat was once a mill. Hidden behind the trees half way up is the town's treasure, Whitefriars, the only complete timber framed building left. The others have all disappeared in the name of so called progress.

Overlooking all this is our splendid Norman church which in less than a hundred years will have served the people for a millennium. The Saxon church which stood there before St John's should not be forgotten.

Church Lane, Hales Owen.

24

Church Lane, Hales Owen.

25

10. Church Lane

This sketch shows Whitefriars when it was row of small cottages before conversion to form a single house. They were thought to have been built in the mid 1300s, some 300 years after the church, and they may have been church property.

The roof of one cottage caught fire and a lot of damage was caused. When redevelopment started it was considered practical to demolish the row, like the timbered houses in Church Street. Fortunately, they were bought privately and lovingly restored, being now listed as a Grade II building.

Currently, during the last year of this millennium, Whitefriars is up sale. I hope that some benevolent buyer will emerge who can keep this jewel in its present state so that it can be appreciated by future generations.

11. Ivy House

Ivy House with its classical pillared porch now
stands alone, dwarfed by the modern, concrete bulk
of Midland House. It once stood in a row of shops
flanked by two pubs, The Townsend and the Malt
Shovel in Church Street, now called High Street.

During redevelopment the building to the right
was was also to be preserved. It was thought
to be a timber framed house from the early 16th
century which had been faced in brick, a common
practice in the 18th century. During site clearance
work a contractor's machine hit the structure, we
shall never know whether by accident or design.
Damage was so great that it had to be demolished
for safety.

Ivy House was the home of JB Downing who became
Mayor of the town when we regained Borough status
in September 1936. The building is now used as
offices.

Ivy House, Church Street.

The Townsend, Hales Owen.

12. The Townsend

The building on the left was the pub called The Townsend Stores which was demolished to make way for Midland House and the big traffic island at the junction of Stourbridge Road and Grammar School Lane. The island was to be part of a relief road to ease traffic flow on Stourbridge Road but the scheme was abandoned.

The George Inn in the centre of the sketch still stands and is a Grade II listed building, which should give it some protection from further municipal vandalism.

The Baptist chapel and the old Zion church can be seen on the far right; both now converted into offices.

13. Rudge's Garage

This well known garage stood at the corner of Rumbow and Birmingham Street. It sold petrol and spares and did repairs and servicing for cars and motorbikes.

To the right of the picture but adjoining the garage was a house occupied as a girls' school known as The Laurels. To the left of the row of three cottages is the site of the old bridge, the 'Rumbow', from which the road was named.

Opposite the garage was a row of shops including Craddock's Shoes, Billy Perks's barber shop and Layton's, a secondhand cum antique shop. None of these buildings remain and the sites are occupied by modern industrial units.

Cottages and garage, Rumbow

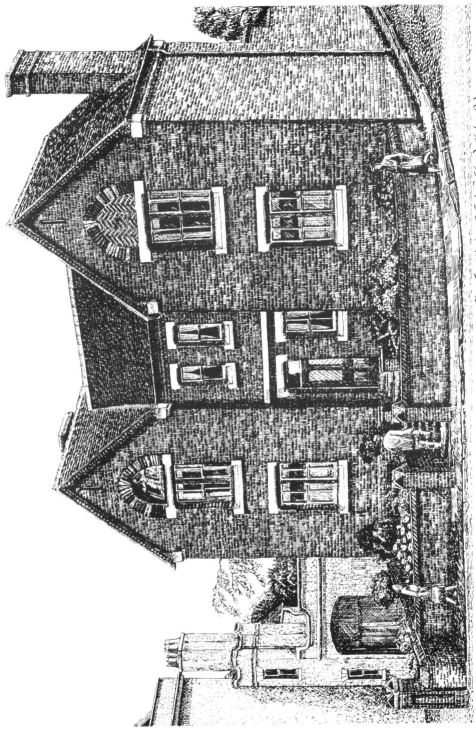

The Institute, Great Corbow, Hales Owen

14. The Institute

In 1877 John Skipworth Gibbons of the Leasowes paid £520 to Robert Smart for land in Great Cornbow. Soon after he erected this building as a type of mens' club or institute with a library and games room. To the left is Brooklands which you can see in pictures 17 and 18.

In 1925 Mr Gibbons and his wife, Constance, celebrated their 50th wedding anniversary by giving the Institute to the people of Hales Owen. The place was managed by trustees who included some well known local names: F Somers, J B Downing, F T Goodman and G F Grove.

In 1938 the trustees applied to the Charity Commissioners for power to sell the building, which was granted subject to getting a price of at least £550. It was bought by a Wilfred Harrison of Church Street, an electrical contractor, who continued its use as an Institute until 1948 when he sold the building to Ernest Brady. His well known firm of Brady Brothers stayed until they wound up the business. The building has been converted to offices and is called Helen House after Mr Brady's daughter, who still owns it.

15. Cemetery Lane

Many younger people will not even know where
Cemetery Lane was because its name has changed.
At the top of the hill and to the right of the picture.
was Love Lane which ran to Highfield Lane. They
were combined to form Hales Road.

On the left of the sketch are the school rooms of
the old Zion chapel, now converted to offices. The
gap between the two rows of cottages was one of the
entrances to the Church of England school. The gap
near the top of the hill was the entrance to the
churchyard.

My father in law was born in one of the cottages
near the bottom of the hill. His mother is said to
have tolled the little bell in the Chapel of Rest at
funerals.

All the cottages have been replaced by modern
houses.

Cemetery Lane, Hales Owen

The Old Nail Warehouse.

16. The Nail Warehouse

Nail making was the mainstay of very many local families until the late 19th century. It was done in backyard forges and usually involved all the family working 14 or 15 hour days. Many of the children started before they were 10 years old.

The warehouses were controlled by 'foggers' who issued iron rod to the nailers and received the finished nails. Payment was by weight and the foggers always deducted a good proportion of it to allow for so called faulty nails. Perhaps unknown to the nailers, the scales were also weighted. They were not paid in coin of the realm, but vouchers, which could only be used at pubs and shops owned by the fogger or an associate. I need hardly add that prices were inflated and quality low.

The sketch shows the surviving warehouse in Laurel Lane where no doubt such cheating went on. It is now used by a clothing distributor.

17, 18 & 19
Brooklands and the Coop

My sketches of both the front and back views of Brooklands will bring back memories to many local people. The house was the home of Mr Groves, the button manufacturer, until bought by the Halesowen and Hasbury Cooperative Society for use as an administration centre.

The Coop seems to have started in about 1870 with a general store in Peckingham Street. Within thirty years the Society was selling drapery and footwear, had built a bakery in Birmingham Street and opened branches in Stourbridge, Lye, Gorsty Hill, Blackheath, Hasbury, Cradley and Kings-winford. My sketch of the drapery shop in Birmingham Street is the third in this group.

The New Model Bakery [HII pg 44] was built in 1929 on the site now occupied by McDonalds' and it was joined there three years later by the Model Dairy.

The grounds and outbuildings of Brooklands were extensive. At the rear were stables for the bread and milk round horses. Wide lawns with trees ran down to the River Stour and in spring the ground was a mass of bluebells, followed later by the white flowers of wild garlic.

The lawns were often used by the Coop staff for their lunch breaks, and during one of them a photo-graph was taken which enabled me to complete a sketch of this rear view of the house.

Brooklands, Great Corbow.

40

Brooklands, Hales Owen

41

The Co-op Drapery, Birmingham St., Hales Owen

42

The Library, Hales Owen

20. The Old Library

Although known as the Old Library this was a comparatively new building erected in the early 1930s. The pleasant smell of the wooden paneling will remind many people of visits.

As the town grew the library would probably have become too small for our needs, but that it had to be demolished is beyond belief. It could have been used for many other purposes but it was destroyed by commercialism in the form of a supermarket known as Presto. If you look at the Christmas card mentioned in the Introduction you can see that in 1948 it was planned to keep the building.

Perhaps there was a hidden reason for demolition. The left side of the building was the old Borough Council Chamber and demolition in 1974 coincided with formation of Dudley Metropolitan Borough Council.

21. Birmingham Street

Birmingham Street was the main road between Birmingham, Stourbridge and Kidderminster and has a long history. It was once the centre for the town's industrious workers in nails, buttons and leather goods, who all operated from their own homes.

To meet their needs the street had its fair share of pubs with The Cross Guns at the bottom of the hill, the Royal Oak, the Star & Garter (in the picture) and The Queen's Head, which is the only one to have survived. This pub has had its name changed to Porter's, but to Hales Owen people it will always be The Queen's Head.

On the other hand, Birmingham Street also had three chapels. The Methodist chapel is in good physical condition but now a pub cum nightclub called Benjamin's. A small chapel opposite was closed many years ago and became a factory. Opposite The Queen's Head was the Birmingham Street Mission which also become a wire factory.

On the left of the sketch in place of the houses was a lodging house known as Alexander Batty's which was used by passing itinerants. All the buildings on the right of the sketch have gone, replaced by a car park. Very typical of today's progressiveness.

Birmingham Street, Hales Owen

High Street, Hales Owen

22. High Street

Here we are looking down High Street from the church gates. The Apollo Stores building on the left, long since demolished, was owned by Major Hackett and occupied by Wimbush's. The buildings of Peplow's Jewellers and Tennent's the Chemist are still there but now used by estate agents who have adapted the interior for their own business. On the right are the archways to the Post Office's yard, Haines Chemist and the old Post Office.

High Street is now very different, having been pedestrianised and with the old Post office and all other buildings on the right as far as Lloyd's Bank in Hagley Street replaced by modern shop units.

23. Stone Cottages
in Gaunt's Yard

Even when these cottages existed you could miss them, for they were hidden at the end of the Yard. Queensway was built right through Gaunt's Yard and the cottages would have been at right angles to the new road and in front of the present Post Office.

In spite of having six doors there were only three cottages. One door let into the brewhouse and the other the parlour. The families who once lived here, the Papworth's and the Morton's, still live in Hales Owen.

The age of the cottages is not known but they might have been built to house masons and other builders working on the more or less continuous alterations and repairs to St John's church. They were in the same sandstone as the church and probably came from the same source, the quarry at Hasbury.

The Stone Cottages, Gaunts Yard.

Hagley Street shops, Hales Owen

24. Hagley Street

Bob Archer's Chocolate Box cafe was the haunt of
the town's Teddy Boys so the place raised many a
tut-tut. Those Teds are now in their 60s and 70s
and most likely to remember the cafe with fond
memories.

The Optician lower down was Mr Chapman whose
son continues the practice elsewhere in the town.
George Bridge's butcher's shop was well known.
but when he moved Mr Chapman extended his
premises into it.

Mr Hill next door was a master at the Grammer
School who unfortunately lost his sight. He had
the fortitude and courage to open a bookshop, a
great achievement for a blind man.

Mary Mosley's dress shop came next. Mary is now
an octogenarian but she can still walk to the town
and sometimes calls in at my shop for a chat.

The majestic Lloyds Bank still looks reassuringly
solid, as a bank should, as though it will always
be there to deal with the town's finances.

The rest of the row of shops, Peache's, Parkes's,
Taylor's and Hawskwood's, have all gone, replaced
by square, modern structures with no individual
character whatever.

25. Cafe and Bull's Head

Walking down Laurel Lane to Summer Hill in
the 1950s, this is what you would have seen.
The building of Johnnie Ray's cafe on the left
is still there but now a chip shop. The advert-
isements had a certain logic. You were advised
to smoke Senior Service cigarettes (see on the
window) then take 'Nip-a-kofs' for your throat
and chest.

Across Hagley Road was Pritchard's, a general
store which specialised in creamy cakes.

Ye Olde Bull's Head stood on the corner opposite
the Liberal Club but the site is now occupied by
a fruit shop. The gap on its left is still there and
provides a short cut to a car park. For how long
we do not know because there are plans to build
shops there with car parking space above.

Café and Bulls Head junction of Summer Hill, Hagley Road

54

SHUKER GARAGE J.E.

CAR SALES

REPAIRS

OVERHAULS

ACCESSORIES

CAR WASH

SERVICE

Modern Private Hire & Wedding Cars

SPRING VALE, HAGLEY ROAD,
HALESOWEN. Phone HAL.1047.

26. Shuker's Garage

This garage stood on Spring Hill, the name once given to the part of Hagley Road where Evans Halshaw is today. It was a father and son business, Shuker senior running charabanc trips while his son, Clive, dealt with repairs and servicing.

Since the place was on the side of a hill the address on the sign, 'Spring Vale', raises some questions. The Shuker's owned a house on the corner of Highfield Lane and while some building work was in hand a spring under the kitchen floor was uncovered. This is possibly the source of the Laconstoon Stream, a culverted tributary of the Stour, for old maps show this area as the source.

27. Tenterfields School

Once known as Tenter Street School, many of
its pupils lived in the overcrowded area around
Birmingham Street. Before it opened children
attended lessons at church schools, the nearest to
Tenter Street being the Mission Hall in Birmingham
Street. This offered education from 1892 to 1909
when most likely the children transfered to Tenter
Street.

At the back of the school there once stood a large
house called The Mount which became our cottage
hospital for a time and was later other things [HII
pg 79]. When it was demolished the land became
a school playing field.

Tenterfields School, Hales Owen

W Hazlehurst

The Shenstone Incident.

28. The Shenstone Incident

The mini and suspected Hillman Minx behind it date this picture to the early 1960s when a lorry ran away down Mucklow Hill and ploughed into the old Shenstone Inn [HII pg 65].

This was not the first time a vehicle had used the Shenstone as its brakes, but it was the last. The pub was repaired, but a few months later it was demolished and the traffic lights disappeared under the enormous traffic island at the bottom of Mucklow Hill. Local people still call it Shenstone Island.

Since the demise of the old Shenstone there has not been another pub of that name. But a new pub is soon to open on Queensway and it is proposed to call it The William Shenstone, after the poet and landscape gardener of the Leasowes.

29. Birmingham Street

This view looks along Birmingham Street towards the old Bull Ring. The Queen's Head on the right still exits, even if it has now been called Porter's. The other pub in view is the Star Inn in Little Cornbow which was demolished in the 1960s. During its last years it became a soft drink and soda house for teenagers.

The majestic building in the centre was built in 1907. Mr Dunn occupied the ground floor as 'Maison Hetty's', ladies hairdressers. The upper floors were let as private flats.

At the far end of the Bull Ring the Council offices can be seen occupying a building called Cornbow House until the Council moved there in 1930.

Birmingham Street View, Hales Owen

The Old Beehive. Hagley Road, Hasbury, Halesowen.

63

30. The Beehive

This old pub on Hagley Road near the crest of
the hill at Hasbury met its end on April Fools'
Day 1960. Its larger replacement had been built
to the side and rear and it opened only 25 days
later, but no doubt a few pints were consumed
before that.

Changes happen all the time and this is another pub
which has been renamed. It is now the Hasbury
Inn.

31. Wagon & Horses

Still standing on the corner of Stourbridge Road
and Islington, this handsome old pub has changed
little over the years. Stand for a while to study
it and see what a splendid Victorian building it
is. This and some other old pubs should be given
protection as examples of living pubs to prevent
them from being lost or badly modernised, like
so many of Hales Owen's buildings.

Wagon and Horses, Stourbridge Road, Hales Owen.

The Woodman, Bromsgrove Road, Hales Owen.

32. The Woodman

The Woodman pub on Bromsgrove Road is still there but in the form of its modern replacement. The old building was demolished at about the time that the housing estate behind it was built.

An explanation for the name of the pub given to me is that it was built and paid for by group of men who worked in the wood trades. The truth of the story has yet to be proved. The building was typical of pubs in the late 19th and early 20th centuries, of which only a few remain in the Hales Owen area.

33. The Button Factory

Horn buttons were probably made around Birmingham Street as early as 1750. William Harris had a factory there in about 1840 and his brother Thomas had one at Spring Hill. That building has recently been demolished but older local people will remember it as a perambulator factory which stood above steps from Hagley Road. It was thought to be the biggest horn factory in the country; there were three others in Birmingham but none compared with Thomas Harris's.

It was to this firm that James Grove was apprenticed as a die sinker. He became very expert at his trade while only a young man and produced beautifully executed work. When Thomas Harris opened another factory by his farm at Kits Well he put his son, William, in charge at Spring Hill. However, William did not manage well and James Grove was put in charge on the understanding that he would share the profits. Grove did turn the factory into profit but was not paid.

Having gained skill and management experience Grove started to save to start his own business and he opened at premises rented from his father in law at the top of Birmingham Street and Cornbow. By 1864 the American Civil War had started, the factory was turning out uniform buttons for both sides and the need for larger premises was urgent.

The failure of Attwood and Spooner's Bank made some land belonging to them available. James Grove bought as much as he could afford on Stourbridge Road and built his factory in 1866. The cottage was build in the following year. Grove was also a pioneer in the development of Hawne Township. When he built Bloomfield Works only a few houses existed.

In 1882 Grove took his two sons into partnership and the firm became James Grove & Sons which is still in business. Grove's rivals W J Harris and Thomas Coley gave up.

The Button Factory.

Perambulator Factory, Stourbridge Road.

34. The Pram Factory

Not to be confused with the pram factory on Hagley Road mentioned earlier, this one stood on Stourbridge Road nearly opposite George Road.

Here Badham Brother's made prams under the name of 'Roslyn' in two sizes, one for dolls and one for babies. We still have one of the doll's prams in our loft. I believe that the firm presented a doll's pram to Princess Anne.

Although the firm traded as Badham Bros., in later years it was owned by the Brown family who lived in the Hayley Green area.

35. Stone Cottage, Hasbury

This old building was probably built during
the 1700s with stone from the quarry close by in
Quarry Lane. This gem of a small house deserves
protection before it is too late as representative
of the places people lived in years ago.

In nail making times the occupants made both
nails and chains in the leanto on the right and
an outhouse at the back. I am told that the forge,
anvil and tools were only removed in 1926.

The Old Stone Cottage, Flasbury

Quarry Farm, Hasbury   Hales Owen

36. Quarry Farm

The farm stood near the old quarry on Quarry Lane. It was owned by the Bibby family who had other farms in the area and still do. From this farm they worked the land which has now been taken over by the bypass.

There is no trace of the farm now, and spreading housing estates have blotted out the rural setting. Fortunately the greenbelt land on the other side of the bypass will give us some protection from this concrete progression.

37. Hayley Green Hospital

The sketch shows what was known as the administration block, although in its early day's it also served as a nurse's home.

Hayley Green was originally an isolation hospital for patients with infectious diseases other than smallpox. Those cases went to the tin hospital at Hasbury. (This closed years ago and the land is now part of the Hasbury Farm housing estate.)

In its later years Hayley Green Hospital mainly looked after the town's elderly. It was threatened with closure in the mid 1990s which prompted a long campaign to keep it open. However, the fight was lost and Dudley Health Authority sold the land for housing. All the old ward buildings have gone but this block remains, converted to luxury apartments.

Hayley Green Hospital

The Old House, Halas Owen.

38. The Old House

This Elizabethan house at the top of Mucklow Hill was the original Pottery Farm. This view is what you first see of it from the driveway, and you can see that it is well timbered. At the rear right side of the building is a small courtyard with a working well, although the water is no longer fit to drink. The back of the house facing the garden is more modern in appearance with a pair of recent dormer windows and french doors. The walls on this side have been covered with stucco and the timbering is hidden. Inside is a 16th century staircase with some very good carvings.

At the time of writing The Old House is up for sale. I hope its new owners enjoy their stay in this 500 year old house.

39. Belle Vue

You would not expect to find a connection between this local building and the French Revolution, but read on.

When the Bastille fell in 1791 a well known Birmingham figure decided to celebrate the event with a dinner. This was Dr Joseph Priestly, scientist and discoverer of oxygen, Unitarian and political reformer. When the news became public a mob destroyed his house, library and laboratory.

Rioting spread to Northfield, Hales Owen and as far as Bewdley. The rioters were mainly colliery workers and the hard core may have been prompted, if not organised, by people in authority who feared consequences from events in France and wanted to frighten dissenters.

The rioters started to extort money from their victims so dragoons were sent to deal with them. A detachment came upon a party of rioters at Belle Vue, the house of Mr Male, which was described as a neat little house near the Leasowes. As the troops arrived the rioters fled but eleven of the leaders were caught.

In 1907 Belle Vue was bought by the Somers family and later sold to the Shropshire, Worcester and Staffordshire Electrical Company who extended it. In due course the Midlands Electricity Board took over and extended again. Apart from the entrance all resemblance to Mr Male's neat little house had gone.

For years the hugely enlarged building presided grandly over the town from the heights of Mucklow Hill. Recently Midlands Electricity decided to move offices and sold the property to the local developers, A & J Mucklow.

Attempts to save Belle Vue failed, all trace of the building will soon be erased and another portion of local history will become no more than words and pictures in books.

"Belle Vue", Hales Owen.

The M.E.B. Pavilion

40. The MEB Pavilion

This neat structure with its simulated timber framing and pleasant verandah was built in the 1920s. It was used mainly as a canteen for office staff working in the main block. Now that the site has been bought by Mucklow's (see last picture) the pavilion will soon disappear.

41. Whitley Lodge

The Lodge stood just off the Stourbridge Road opposite where Whitley Avenue is today. It was a smallholding and sold home grown vegetables and garden plants. My father in law lived in George Road and got most of his plants there.

I don't know whether it was originally a lodge to a bigger house. The only large one nearby is Hawne House, home of the Attwood family.

Witley Lodge. Hales Owen

Giddy Bridge, Furnace, Hales Owen.

87

42. Giddy Bridge

This bridge crossed the River Stour at the bottom of Furnace Hill. When the road was widened it was replaced by a modern structure.

The name is probably a very local nickname because the only person I know who remembers it is the lady who lent me the old photo-postcard to draw from. No one else may recollect the name, but even from the new bridge it is quite a drop over the railings.

You can still see the remains of the weir which once provided a head of water to power a small button factory. Before that it served a forge which may have been one of Lord Dudley's.

43. Coombes Wood Colliery

This was the biggest pit in the Hales Owen area and generated its own electricity. In its early years it was known to local people as The Golden Orchard. It was a modern mine started in 1910, although coal had been found nearby since the reign of Edward I. Coombs Wood reached its peak working around 1920 when employing about 550 workers underground and 150 on the surface, but from that time there was a gradual decline.

In 1948 when most mines were taken over by the National Coal Board, Coombes Wood remained in private hands and worked under licence from the Board. It closed its gates in 1953.

There was a road off Dudley Road called Golden Orchard Lane which the miners used to reach the pit. This was where Hereward Rise near MAKRO is today. Because it was so steep the miners called it The Incline.

Coombs Wood Colliery

The Rose and Crown, Hacken Hill c.1880

44. The Rose & Crown

Haden Hill is not actually within Hales Owen but
is near enough to justify this picture. Since it is
on the steep hill towards Dudley the Rose &
Crown must have been a welcome resting place
for travellers.

The sketch was made from a photograph which was
lent to me. It was taken in 1880 and I believe was
found in some old church files at St John's. There
is still a pub of this name at the same place but
it is a much later building.

45. Illey Viaduct

I have called this sketch the Illey Viaduct but it also is known by other names, Frankley Dell and Dowery Dell being two of them.

The first part of the line was built by the Great Western Railway and ran from Old Hill to Hales Owen. In 1883 it was extended by the Midland Railway (later LMS) via Hunnington, where it served the Blue Bird Toffee factory, and Longbridge for the Austin Motor works, to Northfield Junction. There is a sketch of Hales Owen Station in HII page 52.

The steel structure, 100 feet high and 700 feet long, was fabricated by a firm on Mucklow Hill and assembled on site.

In 1948 both parts of the line came under the same ownership when all railway companies were taken over by British Railways. The last train to cross the viaduct ran on the first Saturday in January 1964 and the line closed on Monday 6th, mainly to allow the M5 to be extended without building a bridge.

Illey Viaduct.

94

Old Illey Mill, Hales Owen

46. Illey Mill

Illey Mill still stands but is no longer a mill. The living quarters remain but the mill machinery and buildings have long disappeared. This sketch shows the house which can still be seen from the lane. The mill wheel and plant were at the back.

The mill stood on the Illey Brook which ran through the lower part of Illey Lane and joins the East Stour before that river joins the main Stour. Many such mills could be found on this river.

47. Gingerbread Row

These terraced houses at Two Gates were called
Gingerbread Row, but nobody I have asked can
tell me why?

Standing at the junction of Foxcote Lane and
Oldnall Road, they were demolished in the late
1950s. The house to the left in the fork of the
two roads was a grocery shop, and it too has
gone.

"Gingerbread Row" Two Gates, Godley

Two Gates Lane, Cradley

48. Two Gates Lane

Auden's Grocery Shop by the post box was once known as Perry's. Directly opposite there used to be a pub, The Old Two Gates. Like so much else, it is gone from sight   but not from memory.

49. Beecher Road

This scene looks along Beecher Road towards
Beecher Street, where I once lived. The house in
the foreground is intact and used as the vicarage
for St Katherine's Church in Beecher Street, right
opposite our house. I understand that the church is
now closed.

Beacher Road, Cadley

The Limes, Gilley Gate, Cadley.

50. The Limes

This was once the home of a solicitor, Mr Homer, and his two daughters. The Limes stood on the corner of Colley Gate and Toys Lane and had this name presumably because its boundary was once marked by lime trees.

Mr Homer was apparently a very good lawyer who specialised in problems caused by mining subsidence, something we still have today. He was also a staunch member of the Conservative Party. He continued in practice to the age of 89 when he died in an unfortunate accident.

A few months later Mr Homer's daughters put The Limes up for auction. It was bought on behalf of the Labour Party and in 1927 became the Cradley Labour Club. This it remained until the building of Wilson Hall, when, to add injury to insult, The Limes was demolished to provide the new premises with a car park.

I hope you have enjoyed this expedition into the past of Hales Owen. My three books on the town have used 130 pictures but I don't imagine that it is pictorially exhausted. I am always thinking about new sketches and would welcome suggestions of buildings and scenes. Call at my shop and pass on your ideas and memories.

HALES OWEN HISTORY SOCIETY
... travel through time ...

Help us travel into Hales Owen's past.
Saint Mary's Abbey, parish registers, nail making, chain
forging, old maps, woodland and inns, we look into them all,
and we have published many books of peoples' lives and
reminisences covering the last 100 years. There are no kings
and queens, battles and bishops here, just ordinary people
telling their own stories - and yours.

Come to our public meetings or join our study group and get
involved in your own history. Help us to uncover the past
and record what is happening now for people in the future.
Our group started life in 1975 when people on a local history
course got enthusiastic and decided to carry on the work,

... get enthusiastic and join us ...

Contact: Mrs B Clayton, 59 Kenswick Drive, Halesowen
B63 4QZ 0121 501 2931

HalesOwen Township Council

- Do you want -
A truly local council?
Someone to speak for HalesOwen as a whole?
More say in planning, parking, highways?
Our Borough as it used to be?
Our Coat of Arms and civic pride?

?????

Since 1979 the Township Council's monthly meetings
have drawn local people into the local issues that affect us
all, schools, parks, swimming pools, libraries, roads and
houses. We try to fill the democratic hole left in 1974
when the Borough of HalesOwen was abolished and
our lives handed to the remote machine in Dudley.
Only when our Borough is restored and in our own
hands can we stop our interests being swamped
and overuled.

Come and meet us - have your say.

on 2nd Tuesday each month
(except August and December).

For more information contact: Carole Freer
59 The Hawnelands, Hales Owen
B63 3RT   0121 550 5440